The Nottingham the 197

Bernard and Pauline

An album of photographs taken as the area awaited redevelopment

1. Arkwright Street looking North. The Continental Food Shop, no.149 Waterway Street, was demolished during the first week of July 1973. The Great Central Railway bridge was a well-known landmark. 25th March 1973.

**Designed and Published by
Reflections of a Bygone Age,
Keyworth, Nottingham
1995**

INTRODUCTION

In 1853 William Howie Wylie in his book "Old and New Nottingham" wrote: *'In the Meadows numerous streets are already laid out, and many houses are at present in course of erection, while some are already occupied. Ere many years have elapsed we may expect to find that the modest crocuses have given place to a crop of bricks.'*

At first, the 'crop of bricks' grew quite slowly, but by 1861 a pattern of housing in addition to a few modest shops and licensed premises, was becoming established. Development occurred, for instance, in Arkwright, Blackstone, Kirke White and Willersley Streets, and in Wilford Grove and Ryehill Terrace. The expansion of the Meadows continued in response to local demand; for example, houses were needed for railway employees and also for miners when the new Clifton Colliery opened. A wide variety of commercial and industrial premises also began to appear over the succeeding years and indeed, into the twentieth century. These buildings ranged from small one-man workshops, garages and builders' yards to engineering works and iron and brass foundries. The construction of the Great Central Railway line across the district also made a significant face-change.

But in the years following the end of the Second World War, it became increasingly apparent that the continued existence of domestic housing alongside commercial properties in the narrow and crowded streets was becoming problematical. In 1968 therefore, the Nottingham Corporation began surveying the area enclosed by the Midland Station, the River Trent, London Road and the Royal Ordnance Factory — which was the western barrier to the old Meadows. Subsequently, the Meadows District Plan was published which contained proposals for a large-scale clearance and redevelopment project which would irrevocably alter the character of the area.

Just before and during the implementation of this radical change (1973-75) we decided to photograph parts of the Meadows in order to capture some of its unique features. We took views of streets, terraces and public houses; we also recorded a number of the corner shops as well as retail outlets selling a more specialised merchandise e.g. butchers, shoe shops, ladies and gents outfitters etc.

During the latter part of 1994, we staged an exhibition of some of our photographs at Brewhouse Yard Museum, Nottingham. We were delighted to discover that the display created a great deal of public attention. This interest was generated amongst a wide cross-section of visitors, many of whom, even if they had not actually lived in or worked in the Meadows themselves, had frequently visited friends or relations there. Since the exhibition, people have told us of how it has revived fond memories of the close-knit community spirit which was such a dominant characteristic of the area. Former residents also remember the variety of shops which gave personal attention and friendly service.

This book has been compiled as a result of the many requests which we have received for a permanent reminder of the Nottingham Meadows prior to its redevelopment.

Bernard and Pauline Heathcote
March 1995

ISBN 0 946245 96 7

2. Arkwright Street at its crossing with Waterway Street. The entrance to Arkwright Street Station is in the shadow area beyond the right hand bridge. The high level platform was reached by a steep flight of stairs. 25th March 1973.

3. The "Star Inn" on Arkwright Street. Waterway Street is on the left. Nos. 53-61 Arkwright Street are next to the "Star", and the tall building (nos. 63-65) is the Midland Bank (dated 1904). 27th May 1973.

4. Westbourne Terrace, Arkwright Street. Waterway Street is on the right. At the time this photograph was taken, the Post Office had recently closed and the business transferred to no.26 Arkwright Street *(see also illustration no.7)*. The fine example of sign writing was commissioned by Walter Medcalf, an earlier occupant of the premises. 22nd April 1973.

5. Harry Terrace, off Crocus Street. On the left: nos. 1-17; on the right nos. 2-18. An engineering works closes off the end of the terrace, a reminder of the proximity of housing and industrial premises which occurred in some parts of the Meadows. 10th June 1973.

6. Corner of Arkwright Street and Cromford Street. In addition to a notice giving details of money-lending arrangements, John Stoppard's shop also displays two sets of traditional pawnbroker's signs. 24th April 1973.

7. Nos. 34-22 Arkwright Street. The Post Office at no.26 had just opened. In this block there is also the "Star of India" restaurant, a record shop (Ben's Place), Audrey's Hairstyles, a branch of G. & A. Warden's (wallpaper shop), R.K. Domestic Repairs and A-Cold Distributors Ltd. 24th April 1973.

8. At the junction of Waterway Street and Mabel Street. The corner shop, no.195 Waterway Street, sold a variety of goods including newspapers, magazines, footballs, toilet rolls and pre-packed coal. The entrances to nos. 1 & 3 Mabel Street can also be seen. 24th June 1973.

9. Waterway Street at the corner with Newthorpe Street. Edwin R. Warth traded as a dairyman at no.160 Waterway Street for at least thirty years; by 1956 the business had been acquired by the Nottingham Co-operative Society Ltd. 24th June 1973.

10. A view down Newthorpe Street from Arkwright Street. This was taken from near the Bridgeway Hall Methodist Mission. The triangular-shaped corner premises, nos. 87-89 Arkwright Street, was formerly occupied by a refrigeration company. 27th May 1973.

11. Arkwright Junior Mixed and Infants School, London Road. Locally this was often referred to as 'The London Road School'. The entrance to Waterway Street can be seen on the right hand side. 24th April 1973.

12. Looking east down Waterway Street from Queens Drive. The first opening on the right hand side, by the off-licence, is Annesley Street. The extreme left of the photograph, on Queens Drive, shows the edge of the "Bowden Hotel". 29th July 1973.

13. The "Clifton Grove Inn", Waterway Street. On the left, Blackstone Street had recently been designated a Play Street where – apart from access – traffic was prohibited between 8 a.m. and sunset. 4th August 1973.

14. Nos 69 and 71 Arkwright Street. Tom Sanderson's Tripe and Cow Heel Shop was well-known locally, and one of several branches which the firm owned in the Nottingham area. No.71, with its pull-down metal door, was previously a hardware store. 1st July 1973.

15. The "Nags Head" at the junction of Willersley Street and Cromford Street. This public house (erected 1860-61) was initially called the "Eagle Tavern"; the first licensee was Thomas Petehill. Abutting onto the premises is a small group of houses and a warehouse. 29th July 1973.

16. The "Porter's Rest", Cromford Street. These licensed premises were built 1861-62. The room to the left of the doorway is the vaults and on the right is the smoke bar. The adjacent tall building was originally the Bread & Flour Society's mill. 29th July 1973.

17. Arkwright Street near its intersection with Kirke White Street East. The "Sir Richard Arkwright" public house was in existence by at least 1858, although the frontage is of a more recent date. On the far right, beyond the cafe, can be seen a glimpse of the Bridgeway Hall Methodist Mission. 4th August 1973.

18. Lammas Street. This thoroughfare ran between Kirke White Street East and Waterway Street. A view taken from near the Kirke White Street end, showing the row of rear attic windows and backyards with toilets, coalsheds and wash-houses. 24th April 1973.

19. The "Meadow Inn" at the corner of Arkwright Street and Newthorpe Street. This public house was built c.1860 and the first licensee was Joseph King. For a short period during the late 1880's, the Ventham family had a professional photographic studio in the yard behind the Inn. 25th March 1973.

20. Junction of Kirke White Street East and Mayfield Grove. The "Grove Cinema" was latterly used as a Social Club. 29th July 1973.

21. Queens Drive at its intersection with Kirke White Street. On the right is the edge of the Recreation Ground which has been retained and is still a popular amenity. 29th March 1975.

22. The "Duke of Newcastle", 126 Kirke White Street East. These licensed premises were built 1861-62. Somerset Terrace, the edge of which can be seen in the photograph, is made up of nine houses. 29th July 1973.

23. Corner of London Road and Kirke White Street East. This scene was taken from a pedestrian refuge in London Road; Cattle Market Road was on the photographer's left. The "Sir John Franklin" public house was erected 1861-62 and named after the Arctic explorer whose expedition to find the North-West Passage ended in disaster. 4th August 1973.

24. A view of Kirke White Street East taken from Queens Drive. On the right is an end wall of the modern police station. In the middle is the Meadows Community Centre, originally a Congregational Chapel (memorial stone laid 3rd October 1872). The entrance to Stanley Terrace is beyond the Community Centre. 29th July 1973.

25. Junction of Kirke White Street East and Annesley Street. The double-fronted corner shop is no.202 Kirke White Street. Further along the street is a hanging sign which advertised a former fish and chip shop. Beyond that, but before the railway bridge, is the entrance to Blackstone Street *(see also illustration no.28).* 29th July 1973.

26. The "Poets Corner", 132 Kirke White Street East. Willersley Street is on the right of this public house which was built 1860-61. Over the years, licensed premises were used for a variety of social events. In October 1892, for example, The "Poet's Corner" was the venue for a Celery Show. 29th July 1973.

27. Kirke White Street East at its junction with Wilford Grove. The corner shop (no.83 Kirke White Street) had previously sold groceries etc., but when this photograph was taken, it was being used to sell second-hand goods. 29th July 1973.

28. No.186 Kirke White Street East. This recently-closed off-licence was at one time run by P. Fergie. Blackstone Street is on the left. According to official statistics there were 114 corner shops in the Meadows Area in 1968. 29th July 1973.

29. Demolition in progress along Kirke White Street East. On the left, at the corner of Derwent Street, is the "Cricketer's Rest" which was in existence as a public house for approximately 115 years. The building in the distance, also on the left-hand side, is Bridgeway Hall Methodist Mission which still remains as an important focal point in the Meadows. 2nd March 1975.

30. Vacant premises of the Bentley Engineering Co. Ltd., at the corner of Kirke White Street East and Atlas Street. After these Atlas works closed in 1972, the business was transferred to Cattle Market Road. The Company manufactured hosiery knitting machines. 24th April 1973.

31. Arkwright Street looking in the direction of the C
run jointly by A.A. & B. Topham. Next door is Thomas Ha
the corner, just before the entrance to Radcliffe Street, i:
at the corner of Muskham Street, is C.R. Groves furnitur
25th March 1973.

immediate left is a newsagents and ladies hairdressers
e shop which at one time sold ballet and tap shoes. On
re mini-market. In the middle distance, also on the left,
the right foreground is a branch of Lady Bay Cleaners.

32. Corner of Kirke White Street East and Arkwright Street. In Kirke White Street, the premises of H. Iliffe displays the traditional striped barber's poles at the doorway. The corner shop, no.107 Arkwright Street, was at one time used as a china and glass store. No.105 is Charles F. Pitchford's fishmonger's shop; next door used to be a children's outfitters. The double-fronted premises with the sun blinds is a branch of Rose Shoes. 27th May 1973.

33. The "Crescent Inn" at the junction of Bruce Grove and Ryeland Crescent. 4th August 1973.

34. A scene taken from the middle of Wilford Grove. Kirke White Street East crosses the picture area where, on the left, is the former Heason's "Walk Round Store". On the right, the "Duke of Newcastle" public house awaits demolition. Recent clearance has revealed the distant view of the dome of the Nottingham Council House. 2nd March 1975.

35. The north side of St. Saviour's Street. By the side of the private entrance door to the off-licence, no.177 Arkwright Street, is a bill-board which advertised the programme at the "Gaumont Cinema" in the city centre. 21st October 1973.

-21-

36. Nos. 156-134 Arkwright Street, between Kirkby Street and Agnes Street. A block of shops which include a greengrocer's, gents outfitters, ladies dress shop, a jeweller's, a florist's, a wallpaper shop and a butcher's. This view was taken from outside St. Saviour's church. 25th March 1973.

37. A section of Arkwright Street. The butcher's shop on the left at no.134 belongs to Frederick Collins. On the other side of Agnes Street is Baldwin House, the premises of H.J. Baldwin & Co. Ltd., – cable cover manufacturers. 15th June 1974.

38. The last house (no.39) to be occupied in Healey Street. In the background, situated in Agnes Street, is the "Miller's Arms" public house. 11th August 1974.

39. A view along Kirke White Street East. In the middle distance a car is travelling along Arkwright Street by the Bridgeway Cafe. Part of the Atlas Works is on the extreme left. 1st July 1973.

40. A distinctive style of architecture at the corner of Arkwright Street and Atlas Street. 21st October 1973.

41. The eastern side of Arkwright Street between St. Saviour's Street and Atlas Street. This scene shows a typical mix of shops: off-licence, glass merchant's, vacuum cleaner repair depot, radio and television store, and a travel agent etc. 21st October 1973.

42. Nos. 188-182 Arkwright Street. A row of shops situated opposite to the New Bridge Inn. 15th June 1974.

43. St. Saviour's Church and Vicarage, Arkwright Street. This church was consecrated by the Bishop of Lincoln in September 1864. It was designed by the Nottingham architect R.C. Sutton to accommodate a congregation of over 700, at a reported building cost of £2975. The road between the vicarage and the garage is Glebe Street. St. Saviour's Church continues its ministry in the present day Meadows district. 21st October 1973.

44. Almshouses in Neville Street. The plaque reads: *"Founded by Hannah Levick on the 27th day of June 1879 in memory of her brother the late George Levick Esq., of Nottingham, who died the 9th day of March 1879".* 11th August 1974.

45. The southern end of London Road looking towards the City. The properties in the foreground and middle distance had been used as Transport Lodging Houses. 30th December 1973.

46. London Road at its junction with Glebe Street. Shows a number of houses in this part of London Road which originally had some attractive bay windows. 24th April 1973.

47. Looking down Agnes Street from Arkwright Street. The corner of Baldwin House is on the right. 15th June 1974.

48. Saturday Morning Shopping. A view at the corner of Arkwright Street and Muskham Street. 15th June 1974.

49. The "New Bridge Inn", 195 Arkwright Street. These licensed premises had a private roof garden looking across into Orange Street. 21st October 1973.

50. The "Greyhound Inn" at the corner of London Road and Ryehill Street. This public house dates from the summer of 1857. To celebrate the opening, fifty guests were invited to a meal which included *"two fat sheep and a round of beef"* provided by the innkeeper, John Andrews. The meal was followed by a social evening – an event which featured singing and *"the sweet sounds of harp and violin"*. 4th August 1973.

51. Welcome to Nottingham; the approach to the City from over Trent Bridge. The land on the right hand side was previously the site of the "Globe Cinema". On the left of Arkwright Street before Boots shop and Institute is the beginning of Turney Street. 24th April 1973.

52. Wilford Road at its junction with Clyde Street and Middle Furlong Road. A view which was taken at 5.29 p.m. and shows customers waiting to enter the "Locomotive Inn". This was a popular 'local' and when this photograph was taken the landlord was John Hutton. The Trustee Savings Bank on the right is no.40 Wilford Road. 4th August 1973.

53. The "Town Arms". A public house which still remains (now called "The Aviary").
The start of Arkwright Street is marked by a street sign fixed to the premises on the
right, beyond which can be seen the approach-way to the Victoria Embankment. In the
far distance is the Telephone Exchange. 24th April 1973.

54. The "Castle Inn" at the junction of Wilford Road and Waterway Street West.
In 1973 the licensee was Nellie Guy. Nos. 19-25 Wilford Road are beyond the public
house. The end of Kinglake Street is on the right. 4th August 1973.

55. A photograph which includes two old-established businesses in Wilford Road. At no.45 is Horace Wright's butcher's shop and, on the far side of the entrance to Brierley Street, Frank Price's fish and greengrocery shop. 4th August 1973.

56. The corner of Wilford Road and Kirke White Street West. After the "Magna Charta" was demolished, another public house – "The Three Bridges" – was erected on the site. The bell-cote of St. George's can be seen on the right. This church remains to serve the present-day Meadows community. 4th August 1973.

57. Simmons Shop, 116 Wilford Road. 'The Shop at the Bus Stop' was well-known in the area. It stocked a wide range of household commodities including glassware, saucepans, pottery, floor coverings, brushes etc. This long-established family concern continues in business at Radford. 21st March 1974.

58. Junction of Wilford Road and Goodhead Street. The corner shop owned by Doyles (Stationers) Ltd. sold newspapers, sweets, tobacco, etc. 12th August 1973.

59. Nos. 122-124 Wilford Road. The shoe repair advertisement was painted in August 1955 by Messrs. Simpsons Signs. On the right is Essex Street, off which is the entrance to Morrisons Terrace. 4th August 1973.

60. Deering Street looking in the direction of Queens Drive. On the extreme right, next to the "Victoria Inn", is the edge of an engineering works situated at the corner of Wilford Road. The uneven road surface reveals part of the original cobbles. 4th August 1973.

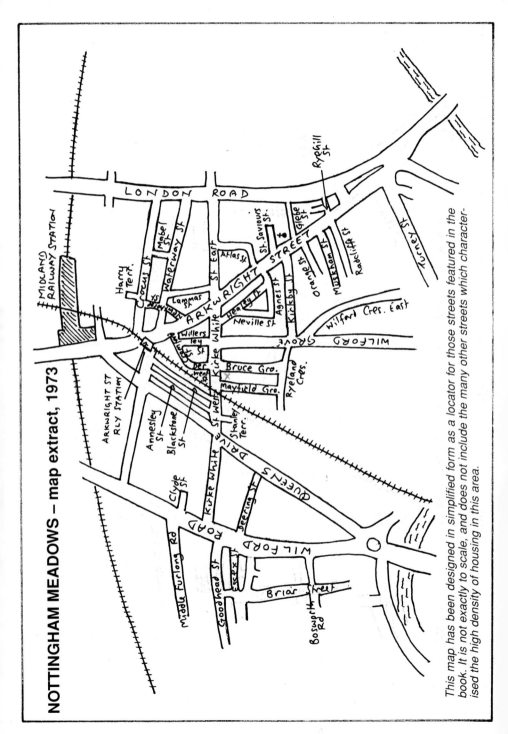

NOTTINGHAM MEADOWS – map extract, 1973

This map has been designed in simplified form as a locator for those streets featured in the book. It is not exactly to scale, and does not include the many other streets which characterised the high density of housing in this area.

To all my friends
in the fancy. —N. M.

Photos on pages 7, 11, 17, 21, 25, 35,
39, 43, 55, 59 are by
Vogelpark Walsrode.

Endpaper photos by
Harry V. Lacey

A Beginner's Guide to
Canaries

Written By
Norton Marsden

Contents

1.
Introduction

Over the past five centuries hundreds of thousands of people have either kept or bred singing canaries. They have enjoyed countless hours listening to the delightful songs of these little birds as well as enjoying their bright plumage and active movements.

Lively behavior and cheerful song are just two reasons why canaries are delightful household companions. Photo by Harry V. Lacey.

In order for the new canary owner to get the most enjoyment from these cheerful pets there are some things he should know. This book will tell you about the history of the canary and about the different varieties that have been developed through centuries of selective breeding. It gives hints on how to buy a good pet and how to care for him, what to do in case he gets sick, and hints on the art of breeding canaries. Although the book is intended primarily for the beginner, we believe even the experienced canary fancier will find it helpful.

The heavy-bodied Norwich is much different from the wild canary. Photo by Harry V. Lacey.

The wild canary looks much like this self green Border canary. Photo by Harry V. Lacey.

2.
Origin

About fifty to a hundred years before Columbus landed in America, the Portuguese sailed to the island of Madeira, which lies in the Atlantic Ocean off the coast of Africa. They found that small, greenish-yellow birds lived on the island, as well as on the Canary Islands

Fanciers breed canaries in bird rooms with cages of this kind. Photo by Harry V. Lacey.

and the Azores. They watched these little birds flitting through the trees and listened to their cheerful natural song and soon made pets of the wild canaries.

It is possible that the little songsters were known to others before the Portuguese. Arabians had sailed to the Azores in the twelfth century and may have been fascinated by the native birds. And even further back, Pliny the Elder, a Roman historian of the first century AD, wrote that there were many birds in the Canary Islands.

The wild canary, or *Serinus canarius*, is an alert little bird and a cheerful singer. He is, however, rather drab-looking compared with the colorful canaries raised today. Adult wild canaries are about four and a half inches long. They are generally a greenish-yellow with shades of gray and black on the wings and tinges of gray on the head, neck, and upper breast area. Their shoulder feathers are a darker green and the tail is dark gray.

Although natural changes in diet and environment affect a canary's plumage, the brightly colored birds we see today are chiefly the result of careful breeding by canary lovers. Canary owners in different countries prized different qualities in their pets and tried to accentuate them.

The Germans were most interested in the canaries' delightful singing, and several centuries ago they developed the popular soft singing German canaries, "Rollers", and also the "Chopper" with its wide variety and brighter song.

The French, Dutch, English, and Belgians were more interested in size, color, plumage, and body shape. The early Dutch breeders, for example, were particularly interested in the size and feathers of their canaries. During the seventeenth century they crossbred and interbred different types of canaries until they produced birds almost eight inches long with long curly feathers on the chest and shoulders. These unusual pets were known as "Dutch Frills".

The English concentrated on breeding small, compact canaries with short, brightly colored feathers. Typical of the small birds they de-

Gloster canaries illustrate the English interest in shape and plumage. Photo by Harry V. Lacey.

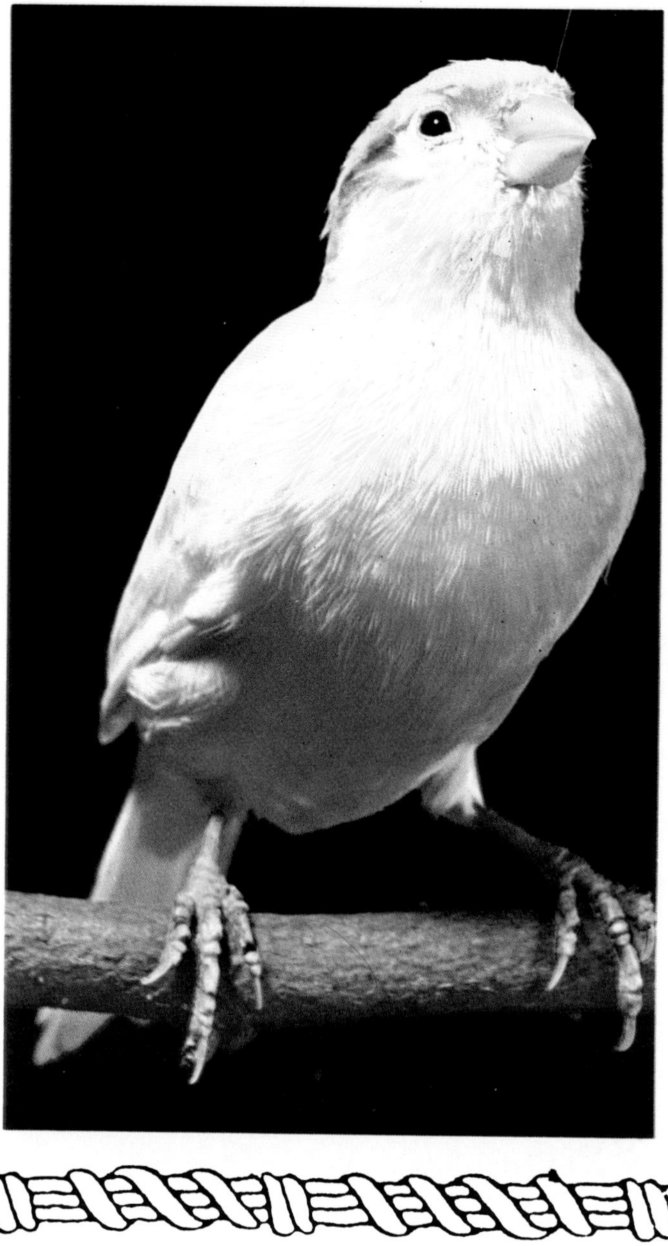

This Border canary illustrates some of the delicate plumage colors that have appeared through genetic mutations. Photo by Harry V. Lacey.

Many people think of a canary as a pure yellow bird.

veloped are the lovely little "London Fancy" and the "Lizard".Later they too turned their research into the development of larger canaries known as the "Norwich" and "Yorkshire".

These early canaries have been used as the basis for the many varieties found today. New varieties are still being developed. Within the last few years, for example, breeders have succeeded in perfecting the crossbreeding of the German canary with the Red Hooded Siskin. The young birds inherited a beautiful red color from the Siskin and a lovely voice from their mother. Only male canaries sing, but females, as well as males, carry the inherited factors called genes which control the bird song.

The Lizard is one of the oldest canary varieties—note the cap and the characteristic markings on the breast. Photo by Harry V. Lacey.

3.

Selection

When you buy your canary, make sure you purchase it from a store that gives a written guarantee as to its singing ability. Often a particularly attractive canary you may prefer will not sing while you are in the store. If, however, you have a guarantee that it will sing,

Some canaries are clear (free of dark colors), while variegated birds are a mixture of dark and light. Photo by Harry V. Lacey.

you can feel sure that within a week or two after you get him home you will hear his lovely song. Quite often a canary has just arrived in a store after a long trip, and it takes any bird a little while to get used to its new surroundings. Your written guarantee is your assurance that you are receiving a singer.

You will see different types of canaries on display at your pet store. Some of the most popular are the "Red Orange" or "Red Factor" type and in lesser number the "Yorkshire" and the "Norwich". Later in this book additional rarer types are described.

Generally speaking, it is only the male who sings. Once in a while a female is found who sings but this does not often happen. The female, however, makes a very pleasant companion, trains quite easily, and many people enjoy her cheerful chirps and twitterings.

Selecting a healthy bird

In most instances the store that provides a written guarantee sells only healthy canaries. A little checking on your part is wise, how-

In Gloster canaries, crested birds are called Coronas, while plainheads are Consorts, whatever their sex. Photo by Harry V. Lacey.

ever. Look for a canary who is lively in his cage, hopping around in a spry manner. Even if he does not sing, we are sure you will hear him chirping and calling. His eyes are bright; his overall appearance is clean and lithe. Avoid one whose puffed-up feathers make him resemble a baby chick.

4.
Furnishings

Once you have selected your canary your first thought should be where to keep him. A cage can be as small as a foot or so square, or up to several feet in length. A great variety of cages is available and the size and fanciness of the one you buy is limited only by the amount of money you wish to spend.

A Red factor canary at the seed dish.

Canaries will enjoy bathing, either in a dish or in a bath house that can be hung at the doorway of the cage. Photo courtesy of Kosmos Verlag.

This wire breeding cage shows how cups, nest pans, and a partition may be installed.

The cage should have one cup for food, another for water. One or two treat cups which fit on the wires of the cage should also be provided for such treats and supplementary foods as song food, conditioning food, live growing greens, etc. These cups are quite inexpensive and are available at all pet shops.

Use a cage cover to protect the bird from drafts at night and to discourage him from singing at daybreak and awakening the household. Canaries seldom sing in the dark.

If you should ever have to paint your cage, do not use paint with lead in it. This can be fatal to birds as well as children. Also, while on the subject of paint, let me say that if your home is being repainted, keep your canary away from the odor of fresh paint. Latex-base paints are always safer.

5.
Varieties

Since the time when people began to realize what wonderful pets canaries make and started to breed them, a great many varieties have been introduced. Most of these have died out because they were unpopular and people stopped breeding them or because they were not hardy or prolific enough to establish themselves. Mostly, however, the reason for the decline of the so-called "type" canaries

A handsomely marked variegated Border canary. Photo by Harry V. Lacey.

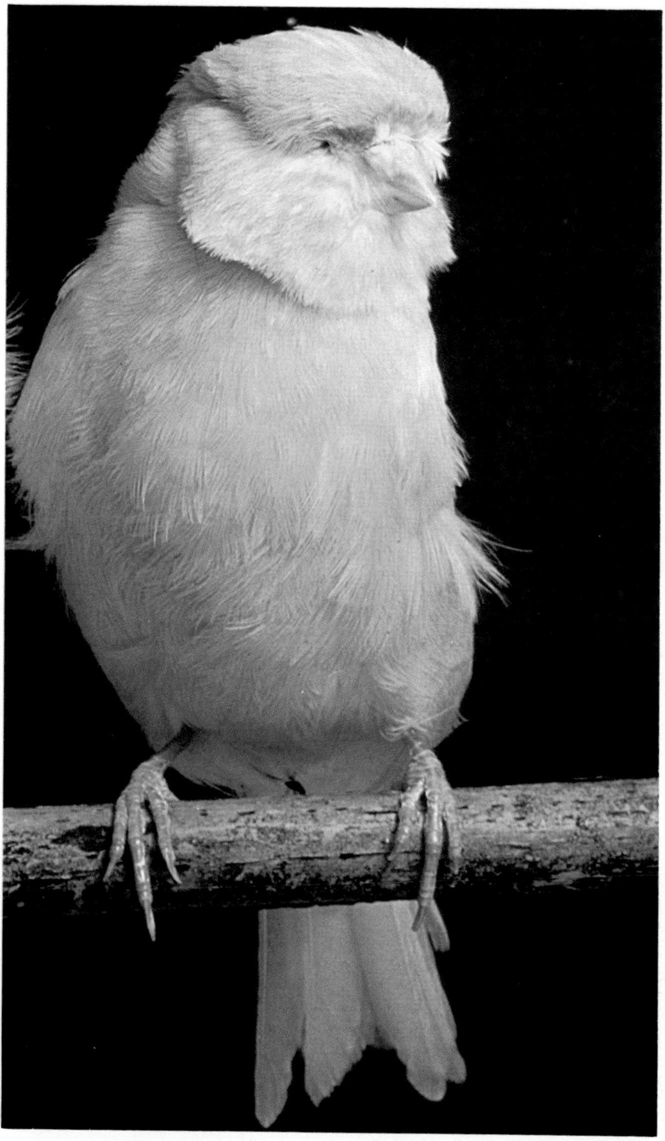

is that the general public was quite content with the common commercial canaries. Here is a description of the commercial canary, as well as of the rarer types raised by hobbyists.

Popular commercial canary

The song of the regular pet store canary is bright and cheerful, with crisp bell-like tones blended with the warble and trill notes common to the "Roller" canary. In most instances, if you prefer a softer "Roller" type song, the clerk has probably spotted such a songster and, since the song is guaranteed, you can safely abide by this choice.

The size of these birds is between four and five inches. Their coloring is either bright yellow, combined yellow and green, or occasionally all green—this last being a throwback to the early wild stage. Most stores also have on display "Red Orange" or "Red Factor" birds which cost a little more but have the advantage of a unique and beautiful coloring along with the same beautiful bird song.

Red Factor canaries: For a good many years breeders have been trying to develop a strain of red canaries. Different colored canaries

Many fancy canaries exhibit full, loose feathers like the Norwich opposite and the Gloster below. Photo by Harry V. Lacey.

The introduction of siskin genes into the canary made a series of canaries marked with varying shades of red possible. Photo by Harry V. Lacey.

The red factor coupled with soft, long feathers produces the effect called frosting. Photo by Harry V. Lacey.

were mated with various wild birds having red plumage, but without success. Then, about thirty years ago, the German breeder Dr. Hans Duncker discovered that the small, wild Red Hooded Siskin, a South American finch, would mate with the canary.

Since that time breeders have tried many combinations of these birds, but only comparatively recently has the strain been perfected. These handsome newcomers to the bird world can be found in all shades, from very light orange or copper to a deep orange-red that is almost a pure red.

In addition to inheriting the handsome colors of the males, the Red Hooded Siskins, "Red Factor" canaries also have the clear, liquid voice of their canary ancestors on the hen's side.

The "Red Factor" canaries are found to be so hardy and prolific that they are no longer raised exclusively by club fanciers; sufficient quantities are raised by general breeders throughout the world, and they are now so relatively inexpensive that they can be found in almost every pet store.

The Yorkshire: Because of their graceful bodies and good posture, the "Yorkshires" are sometimes called the "gentlemen of the canary world". They were first developed about a hundred years ago and have been popular ever since. Many years ago it was said that a good "Yorkshire" can be passed through a wedding ring. The "Yorkshires" of today are not quite so slim. They are hardy birds, suitable for newcomers to the hobby of raising canaries. The largest of them, a good male, may measure ten inches from beak to tail tip. They perch at a 45° angle and the body, which is chesty, tapers down to a slim tail and resembles a streamlined tear drop.

The Norwich: The "Norwich" canaries though heavier and more robust are not quite as free breeders as the "Border Fancies". They probably originated in the city of Norwich, England. One interesting variation of the "Norwich" is the "Crested Norwich" or "Gloucester". This canary has a saucer-shaped "hat" of head feathers. These head feathers or crest may also be bred into some other varieties.

Frills: "Frills" are large birds, up to eight inches long, first bred, most probably, in Holland. They are different from all other canaries because they have long, curly feathers that seem to grow "inside out". They are easy to breed and are good parents to their young. "Frills" are a good choice for the beginner who wants to raise canaries that are really distinctive.

The Border Fancy: These are quite popular among type breeders of today. "Border Fancies" are small for English birds and are very hardy and prolific. They are, therefore, good birds for the novice to breed. They are called "Border Fancies" because they were first bred in the counties along the border between England and Scotland.

Lizard: "Lizard" canaries are one of the oldest types still raised today. Profitable breeding of "Lizards" requires great care, and it is not recommended for the newcomer. One interesting thing about these birds is that they are in their brightest color during their first year. They are not entered in shows when over a year old because their feathers are too dull.

A variegated green cinnamon Border cock. Photo by Harry V. Lacey.

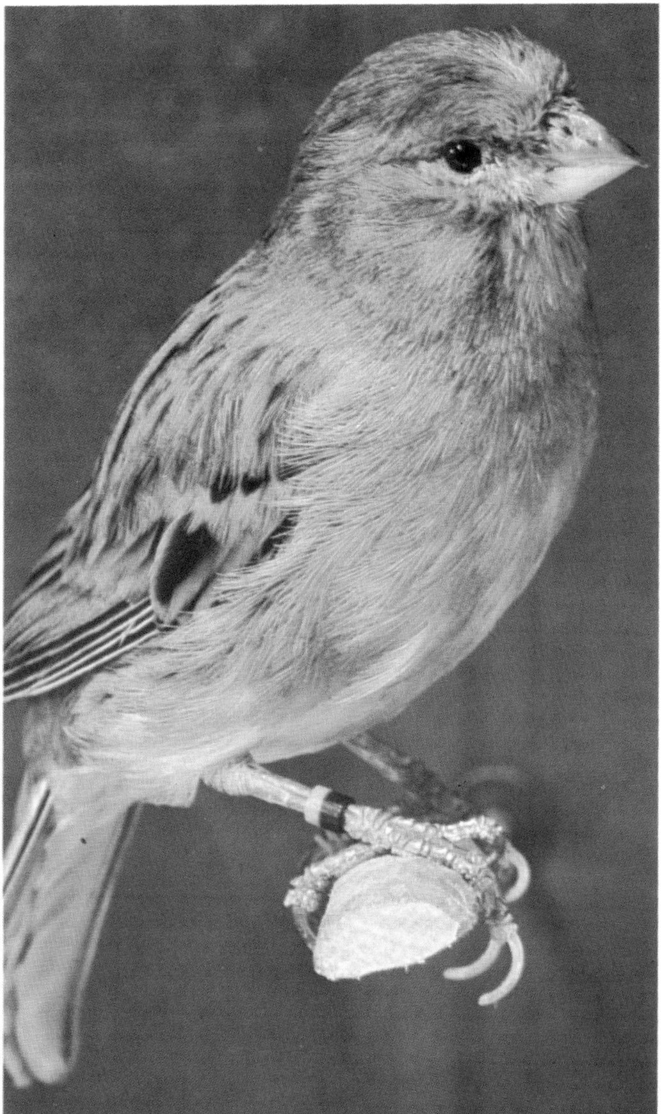

The unusual coloration of this silver brown phaeo-ino results from a combination of several genetic mutations. Photo by M. M. Vriends.

In this frosted rose ivory the red color is diminished to a delicate pastel. Photo by Harry V. Lacey.

Belgian and Scottish Fancies or Slims: Unusual shape is the keynote of these canaries. They are long, thin birds with shallow chests and long necks and tail feathers. They stand with their heads sticking forward from their bodies or drooping down, so that they form a half-circle. They have never become too popular, probably because people are unaccustomed to their unusual shape.

The Roller canary: While most other varieties of canaries are bred for color or form, the "Roller" is bred for its soft, distinctive voice. Many bird lovers enjoy the sweet rolls or "tours" of the "Roller"; considerable training and practice are required, however, to perfect this song.

Once again, you must remember the "Roller's" song is much softer than the bright and varied song most people today demand of their canaries. So before you start buying them, make sure that theirs is a song you prefer.

6.
Care

Privacy at first: When you get a new pet it is only natural to want to start playing with him, talking to him, and showing him to all your friends, but you must resist this temptation for a couple of days and give your new canary quiet and privacy. After all, he has just been through a disturbing experience. He has been taken from his comfortable cage and friends at the pet shop, put into a tiny dark box, and brought to a strange place.

A Yorkshire canary. Photo by Harry V. Lacey.

Canaries must be handled gently but firmly; they are not inclined to bite. Photo by Mervin F. Roberts.

When you first get him home try to let him enter his new cage all by himself. Put the open end of his traveling box against the open door and leave it there until he hops in. If he refuses to budge, then pick him up gently and place him inside. Remember—gently. Put your hand down around him from the back, covering his wings but leaving his feet free to move.

As soon as he has become accustomed to his new surroundings you'll know it by his cheerful song. Be certain that no drafts reach his cage; they will make him uncomfortable. Just like you, he wants sunshine and brightness. Like you too, he cannot stand the hot summer sun, so provide some shade over most of his cage during the heat of summer.

Mealtime: Your bird will need a balanced diet. His meals should consist mainly of a daily seed mixture, supplementary foods, treat foods, and plenty of fresh water. The best seed mixture consists primarily of canary, rape, and smaller quantities of other assorted seeds that give your pet a variety of flavors and extra food values. Give him a fresh portion daily and be sure to give him enough!

Supplementary foods: Canary lovers have found their pets appreciate and thrive on supplementary foods that build up their resis-

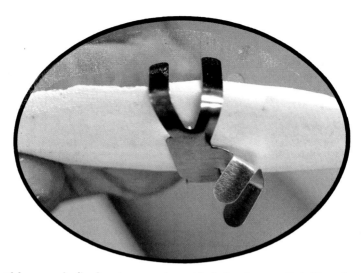

Cuttlebone can be fixed to the cage wires with the bracket supplied. Photo by Dr. Herbert R. Axelrod.

tance against sickness. Certain wild seeds are so appetizing that their discovery is a signal for your canary to start a song concert. Commercial bird foods provide such supplementary treats in the form of conditioning foods, song foods, molting foods, oat and groat mixtures, etc.

Most breeders have also discovered the value of eggs. A convenient way to provide the benefits of fresh egg is the commercially prepared egg biscuit food. All these supplementary foods are given to the bird in the special "treat" cups already noted.

Treats: Most canaries also relish special treats like biscuits or tidbits, which are actually a mixture of various seeds cooked with honey. Fresh greens can be grown from millet seeds in little plastic cups that fit on the side of the cage. Occasionally a bit of dandelion green can be given. The benefits of many fruits are provided in certain commercial mixtures which supply them in dehydrated form along with seeds.

Cuttlebone: Cuttlebone is the skeleton of the squid, or cuttlefish. It provides needed minerals and salts to round out the canary's diet. By pecking at the cuttlebone, your pet can keep his beak trimmed. You will need to replace the cuttlebone about once a month.

And plenty of water: Canaries love fresh water and they drink quite a lot, so be sure your bird gets plenty every day. Never leave him without fresh water. During the hot summer months it is best to give fresh water twice a day, and, of course, from a clean cup. Wash the cup regularly so that it stays clean and sparkling.

Keeping clean: Your canary likes to keep himself clean and he likes to live in a clean house. In addition to making him comfortable and happy, cleanliness protects his health. In summer, give him the pleasure of a good clean bath three or four times a week, or even daily if you wish. In winter, once a week is enough, but none at all if the room is chilly.

It may be wise to buy a little bath for him, one that can be attached to the side of the cage across the door. You can also use a shallow bowl on the floor of his cage, putting about 1/2 inch of lukewarm water in it. If he is hesitant about bathing, splash a little of the water on him as you set his bath down.

Housekeeper: Your canary depends upon you for his housekeeping. Cage cleaning must be done at least every other day. The floor of the cage should always be covered with gravel paper and a thin layer of bird gravel, just enough to hold the droppings. After you've cleaned out the dirty gravel, put down fresh paper and sprinkle fresh gravel. Paper makes it easier for you to keep the cage clean, and at the same time prevents your canary from having to walk on the cold cage floor. Always use gravel in his cage, not sand, as canaries need to eat grit to help them digest their food.

Since your canary spends so much time standing on his perches, they should be cleaned when you clean the cage bottom. An inexpensive perch brush will clean them very well without having to use water. If you do wash them, dry them thoroughly in the oven before replacing them in the cage.

About once a week give his cage a little extra attention. Clean the wires with a damp cloth or scrub them with soapy water, then spray with a mild canary disinfectant to keep away mites and insect pests. Make sure the cage is dry before you return the canary.

7.
Ailments

Canaries are hardy birds. If your canary is properly cared for he will live a happy, contented life, filling your home with song. His resistance to disease goes hand-in-hand with good care and proper feeding. Here are a few of the most frequently encountered ailments of the canary, their symptoms and treatment.

Always keep a sick bird especially warm, about 85°F. Do be careful not to go above 90°F. or the cure may kill him. This 85°F. temperature should be maintained night and day until he is completely cured.

Colds: *Symptoms:* The bird looks puffed up and listless, shivers and occasionally sneezes. An early symptom is a slight watery discharge from the nose. Droppings are white and watery. *Treatment:* Keep 85°F. warm. Some of the softer supplementary foods like the conditioner or egg biscuit should be moistened with a commercially prepared liquid tonic available at pet counters. If the bird stays on the floor of the cage quite a bit, food and water cups should be placed close to him.

Constipation: *Symptoms:* Infrequent and hard droppings. Bird appears unable to evacuate without jerky tail movements and apparent discomfort. General listlessness. *Treatment:* Add more greens to the diet. If the constipation is severe, give your bird one drop of mineral oil with a medicine dropper. Allow more exercise.

Diarrhea: *Symptoms:* Loose droppings with large portion of white matter. Vent feathers slightly wet at first, then more and more soiled. The bird will be inactive and sit with ruffled feathers. *Treatment:* Withhold green foods for a few days, feeding him entirely on seed. Some experts recommend fresh buttermilk instead of drinking water during intestinal troubles.

Asthma: Asthma may be caused by drafts and bad ventilation of breeding rooms, but the most common cause is a dirty cage that permits the bird to breathe dust, which inflames the respiratory organs. *Symptoms:* Breathes laboriously, gasping for air. Each breath may be accompanied by wheezing or squeaking. *Treatment:* The same as for colds.

Baldness: Sometimes baldness may be caused by mites, so, if you find them, follow the treatment under parasites. If the cage is kept too near a radiator or stove this also could cause baldness and shedding. Remove it at once to a more moderate temperature.

Sore eyes: *Symptoms:* Your pet may start rubbing the sides of his head against his perch or his cage. Eyelids and eyes become inflamed and reddish. *Treatment:* Wash with a mild pet eyewash solution.

The bird's back shows the "scales" that give the Lizard its name; the other bird is a Red factor.

Sore feet: If you care for your pet properly he is unlikely to get sore feet. *Symptoms:* The legs become red and scaly. The main cause is a dirty cage. Other causes are rough perches and scale mites. Prevention is the answer here. Provide good care and treatment will not be needed. *Treatment:* Wash your pet's feet in warm water. Apply bird skin salve or a very thin layer of petroleum jelly.

Bird accidents: Dislocation of toe joints, broken legs, or similar injuries are mainly caused by birds that are frightened and panic in their cages. When they thrash about in fright they are likely to catch their feet in a crack or crevice. *Treatment:* (As recommended by L. E. Fisher, D.V.M., Director, Lincoln Park Zoo.) Fracture repair for broken leg: Stretch the leg straight from the body by holding the toes with gentle traction outward. Using 1/2-inch wide adhesive tape, place it behind the areas of the break and then in front, letting the edges stick together. Make several turns of the tape around the leg, then trim away any excess tape, leaving about 1⁄8-inch at each side of the leg. Leave on for approximately ten days. If the break is in the thigh area, high up on the leg next to the body, pull the leg up in a sitting-leg position and tape it to the body for approximately ten days.

Fracture repair for broken wing: Place the wing in its natural position next to the body. Take a short strip of 1⁄4-inch wide adhesive tape and tape the wing ends together at the back of the body. After the wings are taped, take a strip of tape around the wings and body encompassing all. Leave the tape on for approximately ten days.

While treating birds with broken legs or wings it is a good idea to remove the perches from the cage, and food and water should be placed in shallow cups on the floor of the cage to make it easier for the bird to get to them.

To facilitate tape removal, use acetone if available; otherwise any tape-dissolving fluid designed for humans.

Parasites: All birds, wild ones as well as cage birds, may be bothered by mites and lice. *Treatment:* You must not only kill the parasites on the birds, you must at the same time exterminate all the mites in the cage. If you find mites on your canary remove him from the cage and apply directly to the bird's body one of the many good powders available, especially under the wings, and work it well into the feathers.

Mites in the cage can be exterminated by one of several methods. Use one of the mite powders. Apply kerosene with a small brush to all places where mites might lurk. Clean the cage with boiling water, then use a strong disinfectant. Replace all perches with new ones. Make sure the cage is thoroughly dry before returning the treated bird to his home.

8.
Breeding

Whether you start with one pair of birds in a homemade breeding cage or with several pairs in a breeding aviary, you will be delighted with the fun of raising canaries and may find yourself with an exciting hobby and a profitable one.

A bank of wooden breeding cages. Photo by Mervin F. Roberts.

How to start: Canaries are bred only in the spring. While many people start their canary breeding on St. Valentine's Day (February 14), it is our experience that it is best to wait until March 1 or even March 15. This is especially true in cold climates even though your home is kept at an even temperature.

Probably the best canary for the inexperienced breeder is the warbler. Warblers are hardy, all-round birds with beautiful plumage and a fine song. If you have a male canary and want to buy him a mate, depend on a reputable dealer to select a good female of unrelated stock.

Naturally you will want to raise rich yellow young birds, but don't make the mistake of trying to pair only the most handsome birds you can find. Breeders have found that the correct mating is to pair a deep yellow bird with a light yellow one. This will produce some youngsters with deep yellow plumage and some with feathers of a lighter yellow. The important point here is that all your young birds will be healthy, handsome birds with fine plumage.

44

A hen on her nest, but not quite settled onto her eggs. Photo by Harry V. Lacey.

The breeding cage: The next step is to provide a breeding cage. They are available at most pet shops, and a good size is 24 x 18 x 12 inches. These special cages have both a solid and a wire partition in the center.

The nest: Metal nests are the easiest to clean and may be used over and over. They can be bought from your bird or pet shop, or you may make your own out of a kitchen strainer which you can buy in any hardware department. Remove the handle from the strainer and fasten it about halfway between the top of the cage and the floor. If you position the nest too high, the parents will not be able to feed their youngsters. Remember that parent birds feed their young when the fledglings lift their heads and open their mouths. The parents must be able to perch on the side of the cage *over* the nest.

Canary eggs may be marked variously. Photo by Mervin F. Roberts.

The courtship: Leave both partitions in the center of the cage. Put the male in one section, the female in the other. After four or five days take out the solid partition so that the birds can see each other. When the canaries are ready to mate you will hear their mating call, which is a piping whistle. Then remove the remaining partition and let nature take its course.

Nesting: You will know when to give the female nesting material because she will start picking up feathers and any soft stuff she finds in the cage. Give her short pieces of soft string or cotton, dried grass and moss, or even hairs from your dog. Caution: do not

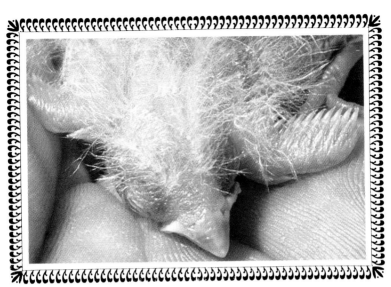

When a few days old, a canary chick is covered with sparse down. Photo by Mervin F. Roberts.

give her long pieces of string because sooner or later the parents or the babies will get tangled up in them.

Egg laying: When the female starts to lay her eggs, one a day, it is best to remove each egg until the entire clutch has been laid. As each fertile egg is removed, replace it with an artificial egg. These can be purchased at a pet shop. The fertile eggs should be handled very gently and placed on a soft bed of absorbent cotton or deep cloth. When the entire clutch of three to six eggs has been laid, remove the artificial eggs and replace them with the real ones. The reason for this is that it is best for the mother to care for the baby birds if they all hatch out on the same day.

Often the female will lay a second clutch of eggs before the first set of fledglings is on its own, particularly if you leave the male in the cage with her. It is possible to raise a second set of youngsters, but if she should start a third nest it is best to substitute the artificial eggs and destroy the fertile ones. If you have not already done so, remove the male.

Eggbinding: A mother bird will occasionally become eggbound. The usual causes are insufficient exercise or the wrong diet. For treatment, mineral oil and heat are recommended. Using a medicine dropper, place a drop or two of mineral oil directly into the female bird's vent (anal opening). Make sure the oil is at the point of the dropper so as not to force air into the bird, and be careful not to insert the dropper too deeply into the vent because you may break the egg.

To apply heat, use a heating pad wrapped in a towel and place the bird on it. The heat should be fairly high—over 100°F. A canary's body temperature is about 108°F.

If, after a day or so, she has still not passed the egg, try to break it by inserting the medicine dropper of oil deeper into her vent. Remove any bits of shell with a tweezer.

Leaving the male in the cage: Canary breeders disagree on whether or not to remove the male from the cage while the female is hatching her eggs. If you want him to sing, he will sing better in a song cage nearby. Some males will not sing at all when they are with their mates in the breeding cage. If you have only one pair of birds, it is probably better to leave them together; in this way, the male can help raise the young. Of course, you should take him out of her cage at once if he annoys the female.

Feeding the young: The parents will take care of all the necessary feeding, but you must make sure that their special food is always available. Egg biscuit food and special nestling food are available at your favorite pet shop.

It occasionally happens that parent birds neglect to feed their young. For this reason it is best to have at least one parent about two years old, preferably the female. This is a good point to remember when you are selecting a mate for your first breeding experiment. If the parents will not feed the young they should be removed from the cage and the nestlings hand-fed with a moistened mixture of the nestling food and egg biscuit combination.

Weaning: Young birds can be taken from their parents when they are five or six weeks old. They often have trouble with hard seeds

Canary chicks begging to be fed. Photo courtesy of Vogelpark Walsrode.

at first and may need some soft food. Successful breeders recommend egg food or egg biscuit along with nestling food for raising young canaries.

Molting: Molting is a normal condition and one that a healthy bird can go through with ease. Although canaries may lose a few feathers all year round, the usual molting time is early spring or late

Canaries feed their chicks by regurgitating food into their open mouths.

summer. Molting at these times may be fairly heavy but the birds should not show bare patches. Usually the male temporarily stops singing during the molt. Provide a commercially prepared molting food during this period.

Experience, with successes as well as disappointments, is the only way to learn how to breed canaries successfully. Perhaps the greatest mistake the beginner can make is to become too interested, too attentive, about his birds. Remember that birds need privacy in

In a brood of canaries, some chicks are more precocious than others.
Photo by Harry V. Lacey.

51

Canaries cannot fly until their feathers have grown to a certain length, but they may leave the nest and move about the cage.

which to carry out their functions as parents. Don't show off the nest, the first egg, or the nestlings to every visitor. Give your pets the proper diet and the privacy they need and they will do all the work. Provide help only when they obviously need it.

We recommend only one clutch or set of eggs the first year. With more experience you can then decide if your birds can withstand the rigors of a second or even a third family.

Two canary chicks with their mother. Photo by Mervin F. Roberts.

9.
Showing

Many canary owners become so fascinated with their little songsters that they begin to breed canaries as a hobby; this hobby then leads them to want to show their outstanding birds at canary shows. Breeding and training show canaries can be an exacting but

Facing page: *A canary that carries itself proudly is a beautiful sight. Photo by Harry V. Lacey.*

Winners at a canary show. The first prize went to a Yorkshire. Photo by Patricia Demko.

fascinating and rewarding task. The men who have bred canaries over the centuries are responsible for the many distinctive varieties that we see today.

When you begin to breed canaries your first step should be to attend canary shows to learn all about your new hobby. Here you will see the many varieties of breeds. You will learn to tell the difference between the average family pet and the perfect show bird that wins prizes. You'll discover that a show specimen must be much more than a bird in perfect feather and good health. He is judged on many other factors: size, depth of color, contour, position, etc. Par-

Yorkshire canaries being judged at a major show in England. Photo by Donald Perez.

ticular attention is given to the bird's head, neck, shoulders, wings, etc. In addition to breeding a nearly perfect bird, the exhibitor must also train his bird not to flutter nervously or refuse to move correctly.

Membership in an active, enthusiastic bird club is probably the best way for the beginner to get started. Experienced club members are always willing to share their knowledge with new members. You can avoid many mistakes by following the advice that only an old hand can give.

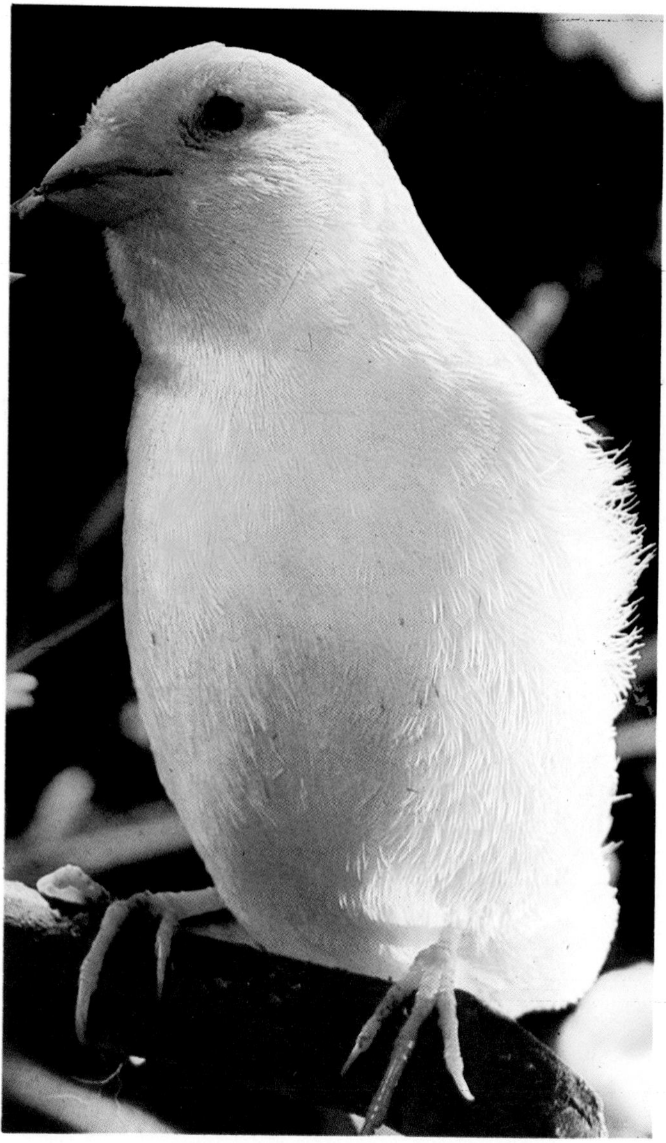

10.
Fanciers

No other pet is as loved by man for song and beauty. Bedridden invalids take heart in the singing of a canary. Housewives pass their working hours cheered by his voice. Children delight in their bright little friend.

Canaries enjoy nibbling green plants.

An open beak means the sound will be louder and, to some ears, harsher. Roller canaries sing with beak closed.

In truth, the canary improves the disposition of all who hear his full-throated, happy song. He never seems sad or cross. Hopping from perch to perch in his carefree manner, he seems to have been created to make our lives better. Just having him around is knowing joy. His colorful plumage and sleek figure grace your home. But it's his song you'll never forget. Your home would be empty without him.

Suggested Reading

ENCYCLOPEDIA OF CANARIES
By G.T. Dodwell
ISBN 0-87666-952-6
TFH H-967

Contents: History. Housing And Equipment. Feeding And General Management. Breeding —Practical. Breeding—Theory. Molting. Exhibiting. Diseases And Parasites. Color And Markings. The Border Fancy. The Yorkshire. The Norwich. The Gloster Fancy. The Lizard. Other Varieties Of British Origin. Varieties From Continental Europe. Canaries In North America. The Red Factor And Other New Colors. The Roller.
Audience: For the newcomer to the canary fancy. Covers early fanciers, breeding systems, heredity and environment, types of exhibition, birdrooms, and cage fittings. Ages 15 years and older.
Hard cover, 5½ x 8", 281 pages
28 black and white photos, 48 color photos

HANDBOOK OF CANARIES
By Dr. Matthew M. Vriends
ISBN 0-87666-876-7
TFH H-994

Contents: Introduction. A Little History. Housing Canaries in Cages and Aviaries. The Care and Feeding of the Canary. A Little Ornithology. Keeping Canaries. Diseases, Accidents, and Parasites. Breeding Canaries. Color Canaries. Form and Posture Canaries.
Audience: *Handbook of Canaries* is an indispensable reference work for everyone interested in these beautiful and interesting birds, from champion breeders and experienced fanciers to those who simply keep a pet canary. Highlighted with many, many full-color photos of good birds.
Hard cover, 320 pages, 5½ x 8
86 full-color photos, 160 black and white photos, 2 line drawings

ALL ABOUT BREEDING CANARIES
By Mervin F. Roberts
ISBN 0-87666-821-X
T.F.H. PS-790

Contents: Introduction. Getting Started. Breeding Strategies. Hybrids. Textures and Colors. Genetics. Diet. Breeding Considerations. Glossary.
Audience: Taking the mystery out of the subject by carefully detailing the latest breeding methods and containing an excellent section on canary genetics, *All About Breeding Canaries* is a first-rate introduction to the topic. The book is of value to anyone who wants to breed canaries, whether to make money or simply to perpetuate strains. Ages 14 and up.
Hard cover, 5½ x 8", 128 pages
32 full-color photos, many black and white photos.

ALL ABOUT CANARIES
By Irene Evans
ISBN 0-87666-753-1
TFH PS-315

Contents: Desirability Of Birds In The Home. Origin And History. Varieties Of Canaries. General Care. Breeding The Canary. Bird Shows. Index.
Audience: For the beginning canary owner. Covers important areas of interest including: metabolism, preening, housing, feeding and handling, and teaching tricks.
Hard cover, 5½ x 8", 96 pages
41 black and white photos, 32 color photos